JOIN ME

in the **BREAK**

Thelma Gage

May you be blessed as you 'take a break'

Sincerely
Thelma G ☺

JOIN ME

in the **BREAK**

Thelma Gage

First published in 2020 by KAD Publishing

240 Bounces Road, London N9 8LA

All scriptural references are taken from the King James Version of the Bible, except where the New International version (NIV) and the New Living Translation (NLT) are used.

Record of this book is available from the British Library

Cover design by *Real Time Creations*

ISBN 978-1-9160249-0-8

DEDICATION

In this work, I honour the memory of my father, the late John (aka George) Gage, whose early guidance has led to my interest in words in written form. He was particular about reading with expression, and the use of grammatically correct language. He was a walking lexicon whose use of big words expanded my vocabulary by osmosis.

I also acknowledge the strong faith of my mother, Sarah Gage, who in her quiet way is very perceptive. Above all, she is living evidence that there is nothing too simple or too big to talk with God about.

I celebrate their contribution to my upbringing and the person I have become.

CONTENTS

Acknowledgments   *ix*
Foreword   *xi*
Before You Begin   *xii*
Biography of the Author   *xvi*

Food   1
    Taste   2
    Watch Your Weight   4
Time   6
    Learning to Wait   7
    When the Time is Right   9
    What's More Important?   11
    More Questions than Answers   14
    Some Travel Required   18
Finance   21
    Heaven's Banking System   22
    Kingdom Economics   24
Security   27
    Bargains or Promises   28
    Big Brother   31
    Safety   34
    Refuge   36
    Guardian Angel   39
Newspapers   41
    Daily Papers   42
Changes   46
    Grace for Spots   47
    The Biggest Sin   49
    Change   51
    Image   53
    Makeover   55

Royalty   58
    HRH Queen Esther   59
    Have you ever seen Jesus?   62
    Simple but Extraordinary   65
Emotions   68
    After All   69
    I Don't Need This   72
    The Sting of Death   74
    Memories   77
    Love   80
    Map of the World   82
    Perfect Love   85
    Reciprocating Values   87
    I Dare You!   89
Work   92
    The Contract   93
    Unfinished Business   95
    Instruction   98
    Burdens   100
    Team Membership   103
Worship   105
    The Light   106
    Powerful Words   110
    Wind   113
    Joy   116
    Wow!   119
    Mystery   121

ACKNOWLEDGMENTS

'Thank you', is a small phrase from a big heart to all the persons whose contributions resulted in the production of this book.

I acknowledge the encouragement and support from my sisters in Christ, Pastor Lorna Beckford and Yvonne Wright, who have already published; my dear friends Sonia Johnson and Nancy Macharia who I hope would follow suit one day, not to mention Rhonda Perkins who often asked me, 'When is the book coming out?'

I have distinct recollection of the awesome feedback I received from my brother in Christ, Andrew Rock, for my first piece of writing many years ago, as well as the technical advice from Pastor Maurice Ekwugha and Anthony Roberts.

Equally important to this production is the editorial input from my sister, Alicia Gage-Wallace, whose attention to detail ensured clarity and accuracy. I salute my nephews: Glenworth Bryan of *Real Time Creations* who produced the book cover, and Lester John for his stimulating critique.

To my publisher, how can I say thanks? For objective and insightful guidance; supporting me through the uncharted waters of the publishing world – I thank you. This publication is testament to the quality of your input for which I am eternally grateful.

FOREWORD

Join me in the Break

What an awesome title, a welcoming invitation to taste and see that our God is good to us.

This book will make you laugh; it will make you consider; it will encourage you to try harder to go towards your purpose.

It instils insight from angles not yet contemplated and makes you wonder, 'why have I not thought of that before?'

As you read, *Join me in the Break* may your journey be a joyful and enlightening experience.

Pastor Lorna Beckford

Destiny's Time Ministries

Before You Begin…

Dear Reader

I am extremely delighted that you have accepted my invitation to *Join Me in the Break*. When we take breaks, we are often alone with our thoughts, away from distractions – this is the timeout we need to regroup after a stressful event or to think through something that needs to be unpicked.

Over the years, I have observed the many times my colleagues with caffeine or tobacco addictions have taken several breaks during the course of a working day. In this way, they find a stimulant to keep them going. I decided to embark on what I call my 'Praise' break, using that time to reflect on situations in life, ranging from encounters with people at work to various headlines in the news.

Admittedly, we may not find all the answers, but one constant remains – there is nothing new under the sun. It is from this premise that I have embarked on a journey of seeing the higher and sometimes deeper meaning to everyday incidents. Our days often follow a pattern: you wake up, get the children ready for school, rush to work, fit in some shopping after work, go back home, listen to the news or oversee the children's homework while making dinner and then it is back to bed.

It is against this backdrop of the mundane and often predictable routine of life, that I invite you to reflect on the exciting spiritual lessons associated with everyday events.

I believe that the Bible is being played out in everyday encounters with remarkable similarities. This book is a compilation of everyday experiences that remind me of something that has a spiritual lesson and of the inspirational discoveries made along the way.

I appreciate your curiosity, because it has led you to *Join Me in the Break*. I trust that you will experience the interplay of the commonplace and the spiritual, and develop a deeper relationship with the Creator and Controller of the universe. Indeed, it is possible that these readings may trigger different thoughts for you. That is equally my intention as part of the process of stimulating the exploration of knowledge.

As a nurse, I was taught that health is not merely the absence of disease or infirmity, but a state of physical, social, emotional and spiritual wellbeing. Hence, it is my conviction that the spiritual journey is equally important to one's all-round happiness. As a manager, I appreciate that staff are more productive when they factor in their breaks. As a matter of fact, break time conversations often lead to practical suggestions that eventually influence corporate decisions.

As an educator, I know that learning is most effective when it pertains to real life, in that applications are made to events or experiences with which the learner can relate. As a musician, I know that the 'break' in the score, which appears to interrupt the flow of the music, actually magnifies the musicality of the piece.

Just as break time provides opportunity for bitesize snacks, similarly, this book presents an occasion for bitesize portions for reflection – time with your thoughts, to appreciate the varied scenarios that bring meaning to the song of life.

It is my hope that you truly enjoy these bitesize opportunities to reflect on our Awesome God who stops by to brighten our days through these bitesize experiences.

Thank you for being willing to *Join Me in the Break*.

BIOGRAPHY OF THE AUTHOR

Thelma grew up in a Christian home and is the eldest of four children. From an early age she was doing the devotional reading for family worship. At home the radio was mainly on the gospel radio station except for the news on the local station. This means that she developed a love for hymns which show the journey of Christian growth and victorious endings to struggles. She is a deeply spiritual person and attributes much of her achievements to having a relationship with God.

She is a friendly, approachable and caring person who seeks to make a difference in the lives of her family and friends. It is easy for her to make friends and she makes new ones on her many expeditions. You don't have to guess. Yes, she loves travelling and she's often on the phone.

As someone who makes the most of her time, she can always be found with a book- there'll be one in the car, in her handbag – in church or on holiday. Her library is extensive and the only thing missing is a publication of the thoughts she has penned. The production of **Join Me in the Break** started as a form of journaling – in that questions arose from her personal devotional readings.

She believes in applying what she has learned and started looking for similarities between stories in the Bible and things that happened in real life – whether picked up as conversations with friends, conversations overheard on public transport or items in the news.

.

This book is a collection of these thoughts over several years and is the fulfilment of a life-long ambition. It is a compilation of 'appetisers' which are intended to stir the juices of reflection and deeper exploration. Some have been developed into sermons that she has delivered.

It is her hope that her reading audience will cross the bridge from the mundane to the spiritually meaningful and enjoy the delights on offer from God's platter of everyday experiences. In so doing, one will have the opportunity to transcend the limits of the commonplace and develop an appetite for things divine.

FOOD

TASTE

"O taste and see that the Lord is good: blessed is the man that trusteth in him." (Psalm 34:8)

"Let's go for an Indian meal."

"No, it repeats on me."

"How about a Mexican?" said another.

"Too spicy!" chorused two others.

"I know a good Italian restaurant; I love their lasagne."

"But, didn't you know there's a new Harvester opened in town? They do a mean steak."

You guessed correctly. We were only trying to decide where to go for our staff meal. As you see, ideas flew back and forth as to what to do or where to go and the suggestions varied according to people's preferences and experiences.

I must tell you that, in the end, we agreed to go to one colleague's home and each person brought a dish. There was so much fun sampling different things and we sure had a good time.

The main vehicle that markets the food industry is word of mouth. When customers enjoy a meal or the ambience of a particular restaurant, they recommend it to their friends and others within their circle of influence.

Strange as it may seem, I am inviting you to taste Someone. He has been very good to me and I know He can be just as good to you too. We have a lovely relationship and we are getting closer all the time.

You only need a sample of His goodness and you will be hooked. He has promised that "all things work together for good to those who trust Him." He invites you to prove Him. Just taste ... and see!

WATCH YOUR WEIGHT

"Let us lay aside every weight, and the sin that doth so easily beset us." (Hebrews 12:1)

Today I went out walking. I was wearing a coat that I thought was appropriate for the weather which was forecasted to be of a lower temperature than the day before. However, as my walk progressed, and my body temperature rose, the coat began to feel very heavy indeed. I actually turned back and changed to a lighter coat as it was slowing me down.

That was when today's text came to mind. It naturally conjures up visions of bad habits that weigh us down and retard our progress. I actually realised that we sometimes have to lay aside some 'good' habits as well.

Weight management is usually high up on the list of New Year's resolutions, and follows hard on the heels of holiday indulgences during the preceding Christmas festivities. Some people actually diet and upgrade their exercise regime prior to Christmas, just to prepare for the increased intake of luxurious foods during the holidays.

Interesting how indulgence in appetite caused the first sin which, in turn, invoked the plan of salvation resulting in Christ's death for our sins. In order to die the sacrificial death, He took on humanity by being born in a manger. It is this birth that is celebrated at Christmas and ironically, it is the time when we commit more sin by indulging our appetites. Some families actually struggle to afford some delicacies that are not ordinarily on the menu.

It would appear that either guilt or actual weight gain leads to New Year's resolutions to make dietary adjustments to improve in the weight management department.

I, too, have made this resolution in years past and broken it in short order. Food is a good thing and made for our enjoyment. However, if we avoid overindulgence in the first place, we would not have to take up a course of self-flagellation or penance after the fact.
You know, I am talking about me.

TIME

LEARNING TO WAIT

"They that wait upon the Lord shall renew their strength; they shall mount up with wings as eagles; they shall run, and not be weary; and they shall walk, and not faint."
(Isaiah 40:31)

Battle for the minds of men started in the Garden of Eden, when Lucifer tempted Eve by saying 'thou shalt not surely die' (Genesis 3:4) if she ate of the forbidden fruit. Of course, Eve thought it meant instant death. Indeed, she did not instantly die, but she instantly fulfilled her desire because 'the tree was pleasant to the eyes and [it was] a tree to be desired to make one wise' (Genesis 3:6). Having shared with Adam, their eyes were immediately opened to the knowledge of good and evil.

God has asked us to trust Him to work all things for our good (Romans 8:28). We only have to give Him time to fulfil His plan. He promised that His plans are for our good (Jeremiah 29:11) and so each solution is in waiting, which is the direct opposite of instantaneous.

Good things happen to those who practice waiting. When we choose to wait, we accomplish a lot without the expenditure of our energies – no wonder we are renewed. Basically, we stay fresh; we appear rested and less stressed because we did not have to make the effort as there was no need to worry or to do anything in the first place.

There are numerous stories in the Bible of how God came through for His children – and His intervention was always on time every time, with a far better outcome than could have been imagined by the limitation of the human mind. His strength is available to us and is manifested when we wait.

Join me as we try to exercise our faith muscles by waiting on the Lord.

WHEN THE TIME IS RIGHT

"When the fullness of the time was come, God sent forth His Son, made born of a woman." (Galatians 4:4)

Normally, an electric kettle takes just over one minute to come to the boil. But it seems much longer when you are actually watching it? That is only because you are frustrated with waiting.

I feel the same frustration at the zoo, waiting for the peacock to preen his feathers so I can take a picture. I am even more frustrated when, having decided to give up and actually move away, that is when Mr Peacock puts on his show.

Just so with our lives. We tap our feet impatiently whenever we have to wait, mentally trying to speed up the process or the person we are waiting on. I have actually found myself tapping my fingers when my computer seems to take longer than my limited patience to send an email – is not that desperate?

Look at Aunty Sarai in the Bible. God promised her a son. Bad enough that she was already post-menopausal, but it seemed to her that God had either changed his mind or forgotten. Basically, He was taking too long. So, she presented a most plausible plan to Uncle Abraham, and her handmaiden became the first surrogate mother. However, the world is still affected by the infighting between the descendants of Ishmael bin Abram and Yitzhak ben Abraham.

So, instead of assisting God's plans, we're encouraged to wait for their fulfilment. He has a track record of coming through just in time, right on time, when the time is right, all the time.

Remember this when you are considering changing jobs or marrying, the next available person, just because you are the only one from your class sorority who is still single.

WHAT'S MORE IMPORTANT?

"And He said unto the disciples, 'Therefore I say unto you, take no thought for your life, what ye shall eat; neither for the body, what ye shall put on. The life is more than meat, and the body is more that raiment'." (Luke 12:22, 23)

The word 'Christian' conjures meanings of Christ-likeness or being a follower of Christ – expounding His beliefs and teachings. I want to extend this definition to that of being related to Christ.

As my brother, He looks out for me; He is interested in my welfare, He is interested in my friends and the things that interest me – all because He wants me to be happy. He wants to go places with me so that we can enjoy each other's company.

He wants to have the same relationship with you, too. I do not mind, because He is big enough to share and He is even preparing a special place where we can all be together.

However, I am not sure that some of us would be happy there. If down here is boot camp, choir practice, undergraduate school, and so on, then we should be practising for up there. Some of us enjoy misery and worry. We are so negative that we become bad company.

Just the other day, I heard of a woman who was diagnosed with cancer and was scheduled for a mastectomy. She actually asked her doctor to postpone her surgery because she was invited to attend a special function and did not think her outfit would fit her as well after surgery. Her vision was limited to the present.
O yes, she is a church-goer or, shall we say, a nominal Christian. Contrast that to the woman with a waistline wider than her bust line, who says she will be transformed for Jesus when he comes for her.

If heaven is where God is and the Spirit of God is in you, then you can experience heaven right here and now. That is what Christianity means – that is how it can be interpreted, applied, and practised. We see beyond our present difficulties in the horizontal perspective to substitute that view with the vertical and eternal perspective.

"Seek ye first the kingdom of God; and all these things shall be added unto you" (Matthew 6:33); that is what is more important.

MORE QUESTIONS THAN ANSWERS

"For now we see through a glass, darkly; but then face to face: now I know in part; but then shall I know even as also I am known." (1 Corinthians 13:12)

This verse compares the 'now' and 'then'. When what seems obscure now, will eventually become clear.

It comes to mind when I am cleaning my glasses. My bespectacled friends will know what I mean when I say that it is hard to see properly when the glasses need cleaning. I think opticians have a special brand of lens cleaner because they are able to make my glasses glisten in a way that is difficult for me to achieve.

However, when I transfer this image to the tapestry of life, I know that there are many experiences that I do not understand fully at the time. For those of us who are parents, we often quote a phrase that we have heard from our forebears: "When you get like me, you will know"; or "You'll understand it by and by". This is usually said when things are not immediately understood.

As a parent, you may recall thinking, "I can't wait for this child to get it." Or you might remember correcting them in a certain way that sounded very similar to your parents before you. There have been times when my younger sisters told me that I sound just like Mommy and Daddy. Of course, this was not intended as a complement at the time, because they did not agree with what I was saying.

I prayed that my youngsters would grow up to appreciate why I did not let them have everything they asked for.

Then, joy of all joys, I have lived to hear them correcting their juniors and giving them the same counsel that they did not like when they were younger.

It sure must warm a parent's heart to see the obscure glasses of youth segue into the clarity and understanding of adulthood, which comes with experience. Then you will have had confirmation that they processed your teachings, appreciated their value and found them worthy of passing on to their own children. What a legacy!

Similarly, in our Christian journey there are things that are not immediately understood. Christ tells us that when we get to heaven all things will be made plain.

Sometimes, the challenges of life cause us to have more questions than answers – "Why was my child born disabled? Why was my partner unfaithful? Why did I fail my driving test so many times? Why did my friend get cancer?" Why? Why? And more Whys?

Thankfully, God promises that when we get to heaven, all things will be made plain – " … then shall know even as also we are known" (1 Corinthians 13:12). I am comforted by the fact that His plans for us are for our good (Jeremiah 29:11) and that "… all things work together for good … according to His purpose" (Romans 8:28).

Therefore, He who is in control of all things and knows what is best for us will make all things plain. Then we will understand the hidden mysteries of His grace and the reasons behind those seemingly difficult experiences will be made plain. The ultimate prize would be a better relationship with God in this life and the promise of spending eternity with God where we will have more answers than questions.

Now, that is something to look forward to.

SOME TRAVEL REQUIRED

Some jobs require that you travel; it could be to other parts of the country or overseas. The standard of the accommodation is measured in part by the company's budget and the employee's expectations of comfort. Comfort would be defined in comparison with his/her home environment.

Hotels are rated by stars. Depending on the country and the hotel chain, some hotels may be advertised as 3-star and be as good as 4-star in reality, and vice versa. Some companies offer the employee a credit card to use for payment (within a certain limit) and others require that the employee makes the payment and then is reimbursed on production of a receipt.

It is no surprise that the person with the company card will choose the best possible accommodation. However, no matter how comfortable s/he are, it will not be as good as home. S/he looks forward to the warm, familiar space and comforts of his/her own home.

Alternatively, the person who has to pay upfront may be limited for choice based on his/her financial position at the time. His/Her budget may mean that s/he could only afford 'bed and breakfast' standard or have to share bathroom facilities instead of having an en suite. Sometimes the service can be less than desirable – from reception to housekeeping – again, it could be a case of 'you get what you pay for'. I could almost hear them comforting themselves that this is 'only temporary'; 'it's not for long'; 'I'll soon be home'.

With my spiritual reflectors, I believe that, similarly, our lives compare to these employees who can not wait to get home to heaven – the place where our faith would be rewarded. I am reminded of the promises of Jesus: "In my Father's house are many mansions: … I go to prepare a place for you" (John 14:2). "Eye hath not seen, nor ear heard, neither have entered into the heart of man, the things which God hath prepared for them that love Him" (1 Corinthians 2:9). I am comforted that, in spite of life's challenges here on earth, my celestial mansion will be waiting for me and it will be more spacious, ornate, opulent, than any other superlative adjective that I can conceive.

I invite you to prepare for that journey. There is no need to worry about being able to afford the fee. Your trip and credit card are covered by the blood of Jesus, so you have nothing to pay; your accommodation is beyond all imagination or vocabulary, and you will be greeted at Reception by Jesus and the angels. I hope to see you there and visit you in *your* mansion.

FINANCE

HEAVEN'S BANKING SYSTEM

Have you ever been given a cheque that bounced? Bet you were not only angry with the person who gave you that cheque, but frustrated that your plans for that money were now messed up. Possibly that would have prevented you from being overdrawn. Does that sound familiar?

Is there a spiritual parallel, I wonder?

I see God the Father as the Banker, with keys to all the wealth of the world. So, if I want anything from His storehouse, I only have to ask Jesus the Son to make out a cheque for me.

The song, 'Jesus Paid it All' reminds me that access to those resources has already been guaranteed. There is therefore no fear of insufficient funds to cover any request I will make. Can our heavenly account be overdrawn? Highly unlikely!

Why then am I so poor? Is it because I have not asked, or that what I am asking for is not in His storehouse? Well, the Bible assures me that there is nothing impossible with God, so it could be that I am asking for something that He sees not to be in my best interest at the time.

All these resources are there to produce in us the fruits of the Spirit of God. So, instead of asking for cash, better paying jobs, material possessions, and so on, maybe we should be asking to be more like Jesus. I think that is when we will realize that He gives us liberally from His storehouse of grace.

KINGDOM ECONOMICS

"Blessed are the poor in spirit: for theirs is the kingdom of Heaven." (Matthew 5:3)

Could this be right? I thought all our work, effort, studying, and all our various pursuits, were to achieve a better life. Certainly, our parents desire a better life for us, their children, than theirs.

The only people who would understand are those who have been poor. I mean really poor. Have you ever gone to school barefooted? Or, did you have to have yesterday's leftovers for breakfast? Have you ever been teased because another child recognised that you were wearing his/her hand-me-downs? If not, you may not understand the degree of poverty to which I refer.

Perhaps poverty for you means not having a television, or a PlayStation, or you are the only person in your class with one mobile phone. Or, might it mean being a one- car family or having to extend your overdraft? That is modern poverty.

24

Well, if all this effort is geared toward having a better life, why does the Bible talk about a special blessing for the poor in spirit?

I reckon it means that my only hope is in complete dependence on God, as opposed to thinking I could attain success by myself. I have had my share of failed interviews – partly because I was rather modest and did not sell myself very well. I have since learned that successful people have no hesitation in selling what they have done. In fact, it is actively encouraged.

If I interpret today's text correctly, kingdom philosophy defines success in terms of submission of self and the elevation of God as the One who makes all successes possible. I can testify to that because of the promise that He has given in Malachi 3:10 where we are encouraged, "Bring ye all the tithes into the storehouse ... " – meaning one-tenth of my increase. You do not need GCSE Math to know that we could be talking about a lot of money here. For some of us, the amount could pay another bill. But, He goes on to say: "... prove me now herewith, ... if I will not open you the windows of heaven, and pour you out a blessing, that there shall not be room enough to receive it."

There is some merit in this, because, I see how He provides gifts and other bargains that take me through each month. Now, it is your turn to put Him to the test. You have nothing to lose and all to gain. He will not disappoint you!

SECURITY

BARGAINS OR PROMISES

As a child, I was often in trouble. I was very much a tomboy and I enjoyed climbing trees as much as the boys did – something my parents frowned upon. Despite a couple of falls and several reprimands, I could not resist a challenge from the boys with whom I associated. If, in the course of a day, my brother and I had a falling out, he would threaten to tell our parents of any or all of my misdemeanours.

He had the ammunition of knowing our parents' forbidden list which would yield parental disapproval and commensurate discipline. If you were in that position where someone threatened to become evidence for the prosecution – you would have done like me and bargained your prize possession in order to avoid the consequences. You would voluntarily offer something that the other party would find irresistible and worthy of their allegiance; these were early lessons in emotional blackmail. In those days, there were no social workers to campaign for children's rights; so you knew from experience, that strict discipline would follow if your action was disclosed. Of course, you would be willing to negotiate. It would range from a toy, to doing each other's share of the chores so that your 'secret' would remain safe.

I am sure you know of people who have made promises or struck a bargain in an emergency.

Ever since Esau bargained with Jacob for a pot of stew, people have been sharpening their negotiation skills by tagging on promises – promises they have difficulty keeping.

These promises would have been made in all sincerity and no price would be too great to pay. The promise might sound something like this: "If you don't tell" or "If you help me out of this predicament, I will" … (you then tag on a promise).

We even make such promises to God. "Lord, if you get me through this exam … / if you help me get that job … / if you help me get better … [the list goes on], I will … " The promises can range from: "I won't touch another drink"; "I won't cheat on my wife again"; or "I'll go back to church".

However, once the emergency has passed, these promises also get forgotten and we soon resume our old ways. Unfortunately, not everyone will get a chance to bargain a second time. Remember Ananias and Sapphira, who were struck dead for lying about how much money they promised to give to the church fund after selling their property, or the teenager who crashed into a tree while celebrating the passing of his driving test, despite promising to be careful? For them, there was no second chance; there was no time to say, "I'm sorry, I won't do it again."

Looks like we need to be careful of the promises we make because, like Esau, we can lose our birth right and set in motion circumstances with long-lasting and life-changing consequences.

BIG BROTHER

"So be strong and courageous! Do not be afraid and do not panic before them. For the LORD your God will personally go ahead of you. He will neither fail you nor abandon you." (Deuteronomy 31:6, NLT)

During my primary school days, children often got into fights during break time or on the way home from school. However, there were some children who you just did not want to have altercation with. Why? Because they had an older sibling in a higher class – to whom they would complain. The older sibling might either give you a warning, try to scare you with a threat or s/he would join forces and beat you up – unless some noble friend stepped up to your rescue.

Fights would be entertaining with onlookers egging on the person they wanted to win. Sometimes one or other of the fighters would turn on the person cheering the opponent and the fight grew into a melee. There were times when someone joined in to defend the preferred fighter and lost courage after a few blows – leaving the person on their own. As the eldest child of my parents, I had no 'big brother' or older sibling to bail me out, so I tried to get on well with everyone.

The scenario that led to the above-mentioned verse was set when Prophet Elijah's servant became nervous at the sight of the large Assyrian army surrounding the Israelites. He was certain of defeat and Elijah prayed that his eyes of faith be opened so that he could see how God planned to deliver them. That is when he saw more horses and chariots than those of the enemy.

This can extend into everyday life – when you face circumstances beyond your control which leave you feeling overwhelmed. Nowadays, the term 'big brother' is used to denote someone with eyes everywhere, who sees all your actions – especially those you would prefer to keep private.

However, the Bible has several assurances that the Lord, our real Big Brother, will always be available to rescue us whenever we need help.

With confidence in God, we need not fear the frustrations and obstacles orchestrated by people who wish us harm. What more can we say but that, "If God be for us, who can be against us?" (Romans 8:31).

SAFETY

"And I give unto them eternal life; and they shall never perish, neither shall any man pluck them out of my hand." (John 10:28)

How many times have we seen parents holding their children's hands as they walk the streets? You can tell when a child is adventurous because the parent may be using reins to prevent them from running off and getting hurt. Other times, you know the child is being carried under duress; you only need to listen to their protests or watch their body language.

In the cosmic conflict, God knows that there is someone else offering a hand – usually an offer of instant gratification and self-sufficiency. Remember the first temptation – Go on! Don't be silly! You're not going to surely die! 'What could possibly be wrong with that?' While God is not going to willingly let the enemy snatch us out of His hands, neither is He going to drag us along against our will. He gave us the freedom of choice.

He offers his hand of safety and comfort. If we get lost, it is because we would have let go of His hand. To avoid that, we only need to exercise trust, dependence and submission to His leading, because with our hands in His, we will never perish. Like children, we as Christians need not know any fear, as long as we are holding the Master's Hands.

That is safety indeed!

REFUGE

"God is our refuge and strength, a very present help in trouble." (Psalm 46:1)

Some years ago, the frozen body of a man was found in the undercarriage of a plane that had flown from the Caribbean to Canada. It is alleged that he was wanted on criminal charges. Initially, he must have been pleased to escape the authorities, but it defies the imagination to speculate what might have been going through his mind as he felt the impact of the changing altitude. I guess he wished for the plane to make an emergency landing somewhere.

More recently, the French authorities sought a legal injunction to close a refugee site at one of their borders, due to the large influx of people arriving there. Britain also instituted a fine for lorry drivers caught transporting illegal immigrants. Police have even been drafted in with special detectors to identify such persons. Yet, people still get through. The other day, some were reported to be found dead in a lorry in Dublin. It was estimated that they had been travelling for days.

Can you imagine such desperation? Or the mental and emotional turmoil that these people go through? Or the questions that go through their minds? I guess that they wonder if they would ever see their families again. Would they survive this experience? Would they get caught?

As world economies feel the squeeze of recession, and unemployment rises within countries, most governments have tightened entry restrictions. Yet, the number of refugees continues to rise as people flee natural disasters, war and tyranny. Some actually prefer to be imprisoned in a foreign country rather than their own.

On another level, a mother makes the heart-wrenching decision to leave a violent partner. She knows it means disrupting the children's education and possibly not seeing her relatives or friends for some time, if ever again. But she has had enough! She fears that he will become abusive to the children as well. So, in the interest of their safety, she decides to seek physical refuge in a Women's Hostel. There, she endures the temporary inconvenience of cramped space, second-hand clothing, toys and furniture, as well as the smoking and swearing from other frustrated occupants. Why? She wants a better future for her children.

When you are having trouble at work or a friend has let you down, is there somewhere that you can find emotional refuge? Yes, I know! I have gone there before, so I can tell you where. *When I need a shelter, when I need a friend, I go to the Rock.* This **Rock** is **Jesus** – the One and Only. He is my refuge and strength – a very present help in the time of trouble. He does not need appointments. There is *never* a queue waiting and His line is *never* busy.

Give Him a call.

GUARDIAN ANGEL

"For He shall give His angels charge over you, to keep you in all your ways." (Psalm 91:11)

I recall hearing a muffled sound while making dinner one evening. I thought that the neighbour on my right was talking to his dog. Then the voice became louder and more distinct. Someone was saying "Hello-o, Hello-o-o". Initially, I did not pay any attention because usually if anyone came to my door they would ring the bell. But I heard the voice again and so I went to see who it was. My neighbour to the left of me was at the door. He was wondering if I was all right because the door was opened. It appeared that, although I pushed the door in when I came home earlier that evening (and I heard it bang), it did not close completely shut.

By then, I was in the kitchen for some time; and over the noise of electrical appliances, the extractor fan and radio, someone else with a different motive could have entered my home, stolen my property or even harmed me. If something sinister had happened, it would have appeared to the Police that I had invited someone in, because there would have been no evidence of forced entry.

My God, my Protector surely kept His word to me that evening. I am convinced that the angel of the Lord appeared in the form of my neighbour. He promised that no evil will befall me neither shall any plague come near my dwelling (Psalm 91:9,10). I am sure you have had similar experiences. Let us plan to be ready for Heaven where we can give our personal thanks to our specially assigned guardian angels.

NEWSPAPERS

DAILY PAPERS

I have just finished a word search puzzle and, in ever-reflective mode, I began to ponder on the variety of titles that abound and how the Bible fulfils each of the following functions. It can be:

1. The Correspondent

In journalistic parlance, a correspondent is someone who writes material for a publication or broadcasting. Come with me (on an imaginary journey) and let us go back in time to around 1310 BC. Let us look at the newsstands on Saturday June 21. All the papers carry the headlines "City walls crumble mysteriously" or variations of the theme. I see a photo of someone looking very much like Rajeh Omar. There are pictures of what was thought to be an impenetrable wall, in contrast to a pile of rubble where the wall previously stood. His article carries details of a seven-day rally of silence – led by the priests of Israel – culminating in the destruction of the fortress without the use of any military ammunition. Do you think you would find this story in the archives of Fleet Street? No! But you need look no further than find the account in Joshua 6:1-20 in your Bible.

2. The Sun

Jesus said He has gone to prepare a place for us (John 14:1-3) and that He will come again to get us when it is finished. In that city, we shall not need electricity or sunlight because the **SON** of God will be all the light we will need (Revelation 21:23). Would it be preposterous to speculate that the newspaper of heaven might be called the **SUN?** It will obviously be of celestial calibre – replete with reports of the saints praising and worshipping God – giving perpetual thanks for victory through grace. In the meantime, while our earthly sojourn continues, we are reminded that His " … word is a lamp unto our feet and a light unto our path" (Psalm 119:105). If we follow its guidance we will not lose our way.

3. The Mail

We all like getting mail, *except* junk mail. We eagerly look forward to the post if we expect exam results, an interview appointment, winning competitions, or receiving news from close friends. Think back to the days of Paul. Imagine the scrolls, epistles, letters that were sent from Paul to the different churches that he had raised up in the Mediterranean and Asia Minor. They must have received his mail with joy. We are privileged to benefit from those letters of admonition and encouragement because " … holy men of God spake as they were moved by the Holy Spirit" (2 Peter 1:21). Imagine an interview in the paper with Pastor Paul in a Roman prison cell. What courage, that he could make such an amazing testimony from death row (2 Timothy 4:6-8)?

4. The Independent

The implication is that this paper has no political affiliation and is therefore not obligated to any particular group. Is not the Bible very much like this? It is not dependent on anything or anyone for its validity – it is actually self-validating. It is the way, the truth and the life (John 14:6).

5. The Star

I do not know much about this paper, but the Bible refers to a star that led the wise men to Baby Jesus. That was a story of a star leading people to the Star, and since then the Bible has been a star offering people direction and light out of the dark alleys and experiences of life. How about reading it and being comforted? I pray God's blessings on your search for the Star.

CHANGES

GRACE FOR SPOTS

"Can the Ethiopian change his skin? Or the leopard its spots? Then may ye also do good, that are accustomed to do evil." (Jeremiah 13:23)

I understand the Dalmatian pup is born without spots. Yet, in the course of time, its computer chip produces those characteristic spots. So, it is not possible to deceive someone into buying a plain-coated dog, because all will be revealed.

Similarly, our text today reminds us that, even if the leopard wanted to change its spots, it could not. I sometimes wonder how atheists or evolutionists explain such phenomena.

Neither can we do anything right in our own strength. Paul recalls that whenever he wanted to do good, evil presented itself.

So what hope is there for us? Well, Jesus encourages us to come as we are (spots and all). He says: "My grace is sufficient for thee: for My strength is made perfect in weakness" (2 Corinthians 12:9). Just approach Him, confessing your limitations and your struggles and He will cover your blemishes with His purity.

THE BIGGEST SIN

"How then can I do this great wickedness, and sin against God?" (Genesis 39:9)

'Who would believe this was going on all the time, right under our noses?'

'He was such a pleasant and helpful man!'

'He didn't look capable of hurting a fly!'

What's the story you ask?

There had been several allegations made of child molestation against an upstanding member of the community. To most people, this was inconceivable. He was seen as a devoted family man with a lovely wife and two well-mannered children; neighbours even volunteered to give character references for him.

When all the evidence came out in court, he broke down and confessed. He even admitted other names into evidence. Everyone was appalled. The question paramount in people's minds was, "What possessed him to do this?"

I know the answer to that question: "For all have sinned, and come short of the glory of God" (Romans 3:23). If it was not for the grace of God, some of us would be in the same situation.

The magnitude of the crime or the social standing of the sinner isn't important – but, that a crime has been committed against the God of the universe (Psalm 51:4). When we see it in that perspective, then no sin is too big or small; there is no room for comparison; there is no comfort in your sin being worse than mine.

We all need to make amends rather than try to save face. What is more remarkable is that the same God who we have offended is the same God who provides the grace and mercy that will restore us as if we had never sinned – once we have confessed, of course!

Simply amazing!

CHANGE

"Heaven and earth shall pass away, but my words shall not pass away." (Matthew 24:35)

It was announced today that the case against Mr X would be reopened because new evidence has come to light.

Parliament convened a special sitting to debate the proposed amendment to the XXXX Bill.

How many times have you heard themes like these? Why do you think this is the case? You will admit that circumstances have changed or vital clues were overlooked. If our forefathers were to examine the Constitution as it now stands, they would be amazed at the vast differences made. Even in our time, things have changed and are changing quite rapidly. Friends fall out; couples split up; politicians make promises they are unable or unlikely to keep, and disappointment prevails.

There is only one person I know that has not changed. No guesses necessary. Yes, it is God! If the case of God versus Satan were to be heard in an earthly court, God would not need a Defence Attorney.

He has proven over and over again that He is love. The principles that He set out at Creation are the same today and will apply to our fellow homo sapiens in generations following. At the end of all things, everyone will say that He is just. Why? Because He does not change. He is the same yesterday, today and forever. My faith has found a resting place, so I need no other evidence. How about you? Are you convinced?

IMAGE

"And the Word was made flesh, and dwelt among us, and we beheld His glory, the glory as of the only begotten of the Father, full of grace and truth." (John 1:14)

In busy maternity wards, parents are not only relieved that their babies are born normal, but that the systems of identification are so efficient that they are indeed given the right baby. I am sure that you have heard stories of babies being mixed up at birth. As children grow up, one can sometimes overhear remarks like:

"Hasn't he got his father's nose?"

"I think he looks like my side of the family."

These statements signal pride in the shared identity which confirms the relationship between parents and children.

However, in cases of dispute, these same statements or attributes become weapons in court. I often wonder why some paternity tests are even necessary. Somehow, it seems as if there is an attempt to delay or deny acknowledgment of parenthood and the associated responsibilities of maintenance.

In many instances, the child in question is the spitting image of the father and demonstrates uncanny similarities in mannerisms, facial expressions or other forms of body language that mirror those of distant or estranged parents.

Thankfully, in terms of our relationship with God, there is no denial of ownership or identity. He acknowledges His creatorship insomuch as He admits that we have been designed in His image. All He wants us to do is to mirror His character. He made it easy for us to have a model to follow, by revealing Himself through His Son. He sent Jesus who is His spitting image, in character, to show us how.

MAKE OVER

"Wherewithal shall a young man cleanse his way? By taking heed thereto according to Thy word." (Psalm 119:9)

Most reputable Department Stores have a large cosmetics section, dedicated to products aimed at enhancing our appearances. They may not carry products for all skin colours, but one can invariably purchase various brands of basic cleansing and toning creams.

There are beauticians on hand to offer advice, demonstrations and even makeovers. They will assure you that even if you may notice spots or bumps in the beginning, this is only a sign that the impurities are being removed, and that the real beauty of your skin will shine through eventually.

For some people, it will seem an expensive investment, so they will only go through the routine in preparation for special occasions. To others for whom money is no object, they pamper themselves regularly, or even every day.

At first, the routine may seem time-consuming, but with practice, one gets proficient and can do it in no time at all.

Did you know that God's Department Store also has a large cosmetic section? His goal is to enhance our inner beauty. He tells us not to let our adornment be merely outward, but rather let it be the hidden person of the heart, with the incorruptible beauty of a gentle and quiet spirit, which is precious in God's sight (1 Peter 3:3,4).

In order to acquire this inner beauty, He has designed a daily cleansing routine. We must seek to know His will through the daily study of His Word. We have to practice the routine as taught and not deviate from it.

We will not notice the full benefits if we omit parts of the routine. As His precepts are assimilated into our thinking, it will become easier for us to reflect His character through the way we speak and behave.

The blemishes of bad habits will disappear in time and the enhanced beauty of God's character will be seen in us. He invites each of us for a makeover.

Have a go!

ROYALTY

HRH QUEEN ESTHER

"And who knows but that you have come to your royal position for such a time as this?" (Esther 4:14, NIV)

This is the signature line highlighting the reign of Her Royal Highness, Queen Esther. For me, the motto is that God can make good out of a bad situation. It also strikes me that life is about risk-taking or standing up for principles. I think once we determine to live for God, the execution of daily encounters or daily victories over difficulties become elementary.

Mordecai's faith told him that God would not allow His people to be snuffed out because of one man's jealousy. He was, therefore, able to remind Esther that even if she kept quiet about her Jewish identity, the Lord was going to provide deliverance from elsewhere or through someone else.

The term 'there's a method in my madness' is often used to assure onlookers that we know what we are doing.

Thankfully, we serve a God who knows what He is doing – even when we can not fathom His plan. There was definitely a method in the apparent madness associated with Queen Esther putting her life in jeopardy, by going into the King's throne room without an appointment.

Once Esther decided to step up to the proverbial plate, she found the courage to say, "and, if I perish, I perish". She was going to speak the king for God and her people. From there on, doors of opportunity miraculously opened up for her that she never knew were there. The King welcomed her despite her unscheduled visit and even promised her anything she asked for; the King had an acute case of insomnia and, what was supposed to be boring bedtime reading, intended to lull him off to sleep, actually exposed the fact that Mordecai played a significant role in preventing an assassination attempt on the King. All of these events put together, resulted in a victorious outcome for God's people.

God's thoughts for us are for good and He desires that we prosper – that we receive bountiful blessings from His storehouse. If we allow ourselves to be used by Him, our lives would be richer because He would reward us just for making ourselves available. When it seemed as if there was no way out for the Jews, God made a way – a way that no human design or artifice could have altered. Just think what a blessing Esther would have missed – the blessing of being used by God.

I pray that we will be able to trust Him even when we do not understand so that we can be used for the purpose of magnifying His name.

HAVE YOU EVER SEEN JESUS?

"Philip said, 'Lord, show us the Father and that will be enough for us.'" (John 14:8, NIV)

At church one day, the preacher was telling the children a story. At one point, he asked if anyone of them had ever seen Jesus. Of course, they said, 'No'. Before he could continue, my then 4-year-old nephew put his hand up and said, "But I see Jesus in my Bible." The congregation twittered and smiled, but the insightful preacher said: "Young man, you've just preached the sermon and we can all go home now." He went on to preach on the golden words that are written in the Bible that tell us just how much we are loved by God the Father, God the Son and God the Holy Spirit. He emphasised the fact that Jesus came to reveal the character of God – something that the disciples who had been with Him for some time had not fully understood at the time when Philip raised this question, voicing what they were all thinking.

I could not help reflecting that despite my knowledge of God and the many evidences I have of his guidance and protection, I have not always let Him be God in my life. I have held on to things that make me worry when He assures me that if I cast all my cares on Him, He will take care of them for me. I have sometimes got caught up in issues that are nothing to do with me and are better left alone, when, if I had only listened to Him, by studying His word, I would have avoided certain difficulties.

There are times when I have missed my morning appointment with God – daily devotional time – only to rush through the day and when I try to catch up with Him in the evening, I realise that the Scripture for the day would have helped me during a certain situation earlier, or I could have used it to encourage a friend.

I am only trying to say that we can see Jesus in our Bibles because He said that He (Jesus) came to show us the Father. I understand it to mean that He came to reveal the Father's character – which is basically His love and truth and longsuffering. So, there is no need to go through life bearing all our stresses alone when He has offered to help us through the journey and ease our load. He says in Matthew 11:28, "Come unto me, all ye that labour and are heavy laden, and I will give you rest."

That day, the preacher ended on a note of hope, noting that despite our separations, bereavements and trials in this life, there is a better land where our journey of faith will culminate – joy of all joys – and we will spend eternity with God. Where else can that hope be found, but in the study of His Word, the Bible. Thus, said the Lord, "And ye shall seek me, and find me, when ye shall search for me with all your heart" (Jeremiah 29:13). He is not hard to find – every word of Scripture affirms Him. You will find him if you only look.

SIMPLE BUT EXTRA-ORDINARY

"Ye are the salt of the earth." (Matthew 5:13)

These days, people seem to get awards for newsworthy feats, or their names are entered into the Guinness Book of Records, following the performance of something extraordinary.

I wish to celebrate the humble goodness of ordinary people who give focus and meaning to everyday living – the people who taught us to say 'Good morning', 'Please' and 'Thank You'; those who go the extra mile on the job, or perform the menial but ordinary tasks of life with dignity. Their contribution to society and civilisation is of immeasurable value.

They will never be famous. They will never be nominated for an OBE. They may never attain an earthly accolade, but they will receive an incorruptible crown where neither moth nor rust doth corrupt (Matthew 6:19). That is the goal of every follower of Christ. Only in Him is there the hope of glory.

Therefore, it does not matter if you do not get the glory or acknowledgment from fellow human beings; what really matters, is that which makes you extraordinary – and that is Christ in you! The Bible says that he who humbles himself shall be exalted. This exaltation will not always come from men, but God has promised to exalt the humble (Ezekiel 21:31).

It is the simple things that make a big difference.

In my early days in the UK, I recall getting a strange look from the bus driver after saying 'Good morning' and then saying 'Thank you' on receiving my ticket. This happened on two other occasions. I mentioned it to the family I was living with. I was told that the driver would not be accustomed to conversation or any other form of politeness from passengers. He must have thought that I dropped in from alien territory, or that I was not right in the head.

However, I kept right on saying 'Good morning' and 'Thank you'. It seemed as if he grew to expect it because he smiled whenever I got on. I must have made his day.

Can you imagine working with people who can not take the time to greet you and acknowledge you exist? No wonder we need lessons in team building or dignity at work. The ordinary suddenly takes on an extra-ordinary proportion. As a Christian, you are challenged not to lose your flavour – otherwise it will be good for nothing. The Christian's charter is to add flavour to the world – "Ye are the salt of the earth."

I trust others who cross your path along this journey of life will enjoy the flavour of the Christ in you.

EMOTIONS

AFTER ALL

"For our light affliction, which is but for a moment, worketh for us a far more exceeding and eternal weight of glory."
(2 Corinthians 4:17)

Is there any such thing as light affliction? Ask the people who were made redundant just before Christmas; ask the parents of a terminally ill child; ask the man whose wife was run over by a drunk driver; ask the wife whose husband flaunts his extra-marital affairs just to hurt her; ask the person experiencing harassment at work; ask the people in countries of ethnic cleansing; ask the children left orphans after tribal genocide; and ask the person who has been falsely accused or let down by a friend.

A man who served 27 years in prison for a crime that he insists he did not commit, had his conviction overturned by the Court of Appeal recently. The case has been dubbed as the longest miscarriage of justice in the history of British jurisprudence. He stands to get millions of pounds in compensation. When I heard this, I wondered if he would have earned half of this amount as a free man. It seems to have been worth it after all.

God says that our troubles do not go unnoticed. Neither do they last long. You may disagree. Look at the case of the disabled child. After the initial shock, parents learn to cope and the child is able to achieve a potential that would not otherwise have been possible, had not the parents grown stronger emotionally, physically and spiritually.

Just listen to the expressions of surprise whenever a difficulty has been overcome.

"Can you believe that it's five years since my relative got a stroke?"
"If you told me this time last year that I'd be going through this, I would have laughed at you."
"Hasn't he managed well with those children since his wife died?"

Why these questions or comments? None of us know the end from the beginning.

No need to worry. God plans to compensate us for our troubles – not that He offended us. He is only giving us a prize for endurance. Some get a taste of their reward in this life – they become more caring, sensitive people, or they become ambassadors for worthy causes. But God's reward is eternal. He is working on it right now. He has gone to prepare a mansion for each of us where we can live with Him eternally (John 14:1-3) and He assures us that "eye hath not seen, nor ear heard, the things which God hath prepared for them that love Him" (1 Corinthians 2:9).

One thing I know is that when we get our eternal reward, we will confess that all the difficulties of this life would have been worth it AFTER ALL.

I DON'T NEED THIS!

"I know what it is to be in need, and I know what it is to have plenty. I have learned the secret of being content in any and every situation, whether well fed or hungry, whether living in plenty or in want. I can do this through Him who gives me strength." (Philippians 4:12, 13, NIV)

How many times has this statement been made to express discontentment with a situation? Whether it is in the face of an obstructive boss, a demanding partner, or feuding relatives – it is meant to convey that the views or behaviour of another party are not in harmony with ours. More importantly, this is a behaviour that we did not expect from that particular party. The pain is greater because of the high esteem in which we held him/her or the relationship we had with him/her before the incident which threatened to divide our opinions.

Reflecting on the life of Job, he never once said this or implied that God might have made a mistake in giving him those trials. Paul learned to be content in all circumstances.

Essentially, God knows the lessons we need to learn to grow more like Him. James says " … count it all joy when ye fall into diverse temptations" (James 1:2, 3). God has promised not to give us more than we are capable of dealing with (1 Corinthians 10:13).

So, the next time you are tempted to say, "I don't need this", ask instead, "What are you trying to teach me, Lord?" The sooner we adopt this position, the quicker we will learn what God is trying to do in and through us, and maybe the physical or emotional pain will be bearable after all.

THE STING OF DEATH

"O death, where is thy sting? O grave, where is thy victory?"
(1 Corinthians 15:55)

I recently heard of a husband and wife who died on the same day at different times. This couple had a very close relationship and their uncanny departure from this life brings new meaning to the clause in the marriage vows – *"til death do us part"*. We may wonder how much pain a family can take, but we are assured that death is not the victor when we die in the Lord. Psalm 127:2 reminds us that God gives his beloved sleep. The setting is one where the house is built on a solid foundation and the city is fortified and securely guarded. His 'beloved' are those who build the houses of their characters on the foundation of God's Word; they will be rewarded with the peace, rest and eternal security that only He can give.

This brings me to a question that has plagued my thoughts. I am intrigued by the origins and meanings of words and have always wondered why the term 'rest in peace' is used in reference to the dead. Then I came across 2 Kings 22:20 where God told King Josiah, through Huldah, the prophetess: "Thou shalt be gathered into thy grave in peace; and thine eyes shall not see all the evil which I will bring upon this place"; this was due to their persistent disobedience and following after other gods.

Therefore, for those who love God and serve Him faithfully in life, death has no sting. We are told, "As the days of Noah were, so shall also the coming of the Son of man be ... They were eating and drinking" and sudden destruction came upon them (Matthew 24:37-39). The fact that God would have spared his children from seeing the destruction that is coming on the earth, by allowing them to sleep in death, is something to be celebrated. Hence, we are further encouraged not to weep as those who have no hope (1 Thessalonians 4:13-18) for "blessed are the dead which die in the Lord" (Revelation 14:13).

Indeed, this brings a new perspective to death; it has been conquered already when Christ was resurrected. I am reminded of the song 'Because He lives I can face tomorrow'. Despite the pain of bereavement, there is the hope of the resurrection to eternal, which is the hope of all Christians. Let us prepare to face death with peace because the sting has been removed. Thanks be to God.

MEMORIES

"I thank my God every time I remember you."
(Philippians 1:3, NIV)

Can your friends say that of you?

Each of us is called to ministry – ministry being any avenue through which we can be God's ambassador to another traveller along this journey of life.

I sometimes browse through the card shops and I spot interesting or unusual items that would make just the right gift for someone. I could imagine the smile of appreciation that would light up his/her faces upon receipt.

Conversely, I experience flashes of conversations past, humorous, yet inspirational emails received, or a shared joke with a colleague (and I am smiling as I write because the memory has made my day even brighter). Or, I look at photos and the memories around the circumstances in which they were taken, evoke a smile.

Now Paul did not have the luxury of reclining in his armchair, looking at a photo album, when he was writing to the church members in Philippi. Instead, he was writing from solitary confinement in the prison where he was remanded – a punishment for his faith. Yet, he was encouraged by the memories from the experiences he shared in ministry with the church members. These memories served to cheer him up while in prison. What's remarkable, is that Paul did not really need cheering up, because he subscribed to the philosophy of being content in all things (Philippians 4:11).

We are talking about the same Paul whose ministry started after his about face at Damascus. If he were living in our day, he would have remembered Brother B who played the piano, the fervent prayers of Sister X, the way Brother S led the singing and the lovely dinners sitting at Sister A's kitchen table.

The Apostle Paul's significant memories centred on how the members of the early church supported him with their gifts, and how they had grown spiritually since their conversion. It was against this background that he could assure them that the God who started the good work of growth and transformation in them would see it to completion (Philippians 1:6). He saw himself as having received their gifts on God's behalf and pronounced a benediction on them – very certain that God would supply all their needs (Philippians 4:19) because of their willingness to give themselves and their possessions to the cause of ministry.

How will you be remembered?

LOVE

"This is how we know what love is: Jesus Christ laid down His life for us. And we ought to lay down our lives for our brothers." (1 John 3:16, NIV)

Love is expressed in many ways. Love means different things to different people. For some, it is a candle-lit dinner, a lovely bouquet, or a weekend retreat.

The expression is more meaningful in proportion to the extent to which one is touched emotionally. Again, different things touch different people differently. I remember going shopping with some friends. One friend made a purchase and we all gushed over how nice the item was. She spontaneously turned around and presented it to another member of the group and said, "It's for you!" It was her way of saying thanks for something the person had done for her. The receiving friend was close to tears and so was I – it was a touching gesture.

I am easily touched by good music. So many songs or hymns are born out of the pain and disappointment associated with failed relationships. But when I sing 'How great thou art' – especially the stanza that refers to how God did not spare His Son, but sent Him to die for my sin, I am overwhelmed to be on the receiving end of such LOVE. It makes me feel special and my worship erupts with joy and passion. I cannot but sing from my heart when I consider how undeserving I am.

It humbles me to know that God had so much LOVE for me that He gave up eternity to enter my time and space just to give me a chance salvation. In this context, I can understand how I too need to 'lay down my life for a friend/brother'. I understand that it encourages me to give up some of my time so that another traveller can enter eternity. That is the extent to which I will demonstrate my love to my fellowmen – by seeing them as candidates for heaven and help them along their journey.

MAP OF THE WORLD

"For God so loved the world that He gave His only begotten Son, that whosoever believeth in him should not perish, but have everlasting life." (John 3:16)

I saw a film recently in which Sigourney Weaver played the part of a very harassed, overworked wife and mother. She had a very close friend whose children came over to swim with her children. While the children were playing in the lounge, she went to change into her swimsuit. On return, one of the children was missing. The caretaker mother found the child face down in the pond and, despite efforts to resuscitate, the child later died in hospital.

Obviously, this mother felt terrible about what had happened. However, this was nothing compared to how the local community treated her and demonstrated their displeasure. People whispered about the family in the street and at the funeral; graffiti was sprayed on their home and one parent sued her for child abuse. The mother served some time in prison, even though the friend testified in her defence in court. She was later acquitted.

When she was reunited with her family, she referred to them as a little circle of outcasts. During all these difficulties, the one thing that seemed to keep her focussed was her childhood drawing of the map of the world. The world for her was the shape of a maple leaf. This included her family and the friend whose child had drowned.

When I look into my Bible, I see a catalogue of people who were outcasts at some point in their lives. Remember Rahab, the harlot, and the woman caught in adultery? It is interesting how Jesus chose to teach us important lessons from their lives.

On reflection, I could only think of another circle of outcasts who have one thing in common. That circle includes you and me. We are sinners who do not deserve to enter God's presence, but through His generous love and mercy, we are the recipients of His grace. Jesus came to show us how to live with each other. Left to some of us, people like Matthew, the tax collector, and Peter, the fisherman, would not have qualified to be in the inner circle. We would be just like the Pharisees and condemn Jesus for mixing with publicans and sinners. Yet, were it not for His grace, we too would be outside the circle, with no hope of salvation.

Jesus came to show us that He loves us enough to forgive our sins and to reconcile us to Himself, so that we, in turn, can be reconciled to each other. Other than my friends and family, my new map will need to include the people who I would not otherwise have spoken to – people who upset me, or whose behaviour I do not condone. I would include them by asking God to let His grace shine on them, like it did on me. They, too, need to experience the joy of a life with Christ at the centre. I stand humbled at this privilege because I might be the only ambassador for Christ that some people may ever see – which makes me part of their world.

Do you need to redesign your map of the world?

PERFECT LOVE

"There is no fear in love; but perfect love casteth out fear: because fear hath torment." (1 John 4:18)

"Where are you coming from? I expected to meet my dinner on the table when I came in from work," he shouted. "You know I don't like you going out without telling me where you're going. How many times do I have to tell you that there's only one person in charge in this house, and that's me?"

Can you imagine the fear instilled in the person being spoken to? Every word is like a physical blow and weakens the emotional capacity for response or defence.

In another related incident, a Samaritan volunteer answers the phone to hear a woman sobbing. Why? Her partner has been violent to her … yet again.

When asked what she wanted to do, the caller said she could not leave her partner because it would damage his career. She went on to say that it was her fault for forgetting to collect the dry cleaning and there was a certain shirt he wanted to wear to an important meeting the next day. She claimed he was under a lot of stress at work lately – and was otherwise a nice man. He even said he was sorry.

She was advised to be seen by a doctor, but she timidly declined, saying that he had not hit her in the face and so she had no bruises to show.

Someone outside of this situation cannot comprehend what aspect of love keeps such a relationship going. Fear pervades like an addiction.

But God says in His Word, "Perfect love casts out fear." With love, there is no threat of violence, intimidation, humiliation or suppression. Thank God that He came to bring freedom to those held captive by fear (Isaiah 61:1).

RECIPROCATING VALUES

"So, in everything, do to others what you would have them do to you." (Matthew 7:12a NIV)

I am sure that you have come across the following notice at some point – 'Please don't throw paper towels in this toilet'. This can be translated 'Please leave this toilet as you would like to meet it'. Now, suppose I were to add the text from Matthew 7:12 at the end of this notice? Would you think that I committed sacrilege? I hope not. This text is basically asking us to think of others whenever we do anything and it can be applied to any of our activities.

This has become the Golden Rule by which our relationships should be governed. Have you ever bought a gift for someone and then gone back and got the same thing for yourself? That is not just because it was a nice thing or that you had the patent for a bright idea, but that you were making a practical application of a Biblical principle.

That is the standard by which we should live – love as you wish to be loved; give as you wish to receive and forgive as you wish to be forgiven. Not that it is as easy to do as it is to say, because some people do put you to the test. However, Jesus came to tell us that it is possible to apply these Biblical principles to our real-life relationships in the form of reciprocating values.

How about starting to practice this from today?

I DARE YOU

"And the devil said unto him, 'If thou be the Son of God, command this stone that it be made bread'. And Jesus answered him, saying, 'It is written, that man shall not live by bread alone, but by every word of God.'"
(Luke 4:3,4)

A: Do you mean to say that you didn't tell her a piece of your mind? How could you let such an opportunity pass?

B: You know that's not my nature. I'm not as strong as you.

A: The real problem is that you're just a coward. She would never dare to talk to me like that and hope to get away with it.

The person on the receiving end of these remarks must feel small, humiliated and dim-witted. Pride is challenged and the ego is bruised.

Of course, in the face of such an attack, the natural response is to prove one's self. We are tempted to show our audience what we are really made of. Deep down it is about saving face, setting the record straight and removing any possible doubt as to our ability to take up the challenge.

After 40 days without food, it can be said that Jesus was really slow on the uptake when Satan presented his tempting dares (Matthew 4:1-11). Obviously, He was too hungry to think as quickly as He was used to doing. Jesus definitely missed a chance to prove to Satan that He was who He said He was. In hindsight, many of us would admit that we would not have missed this opportunity. There could not be anything wrong in proving that we were on God's side.

I am reminded that it was because of pride that Lucifer lost his place in heaven and, since his eviction to planet Earth, he has used the subtleties of semantics to plant doubt in people's minds and prey upon their pride. Jesus showed us that if we are truly connected to the Father, we can be so aware of Satan's ploys, that we do not have to bite the bait of temptation – even when our blood sugar is low and our brains feel scrambled from fatigue. Had Jesus jumped at the opportunity to prove Himself and taken up the dare, He would have given Satan the victory. Essentially, He might have won the dare, but He would have lost the war.

Instead, with a simple, "It is written!" Jesus not only vindicated God's character and existence, but He had the last laugh, and He advises us to follow His example: "Study to show thyself approved unto God, a workman that needeth not to be ashamed, rightly dividing the word of truth" (2 Timothy 2:15).

WORK

THE CONTRACT

"I will establish my covenant as an everlasting covenant between me and you and your descendants after you for the generations to come, to be your God and the God of your descendants after you." (Genesis 17:7, NIV)

I remember that when I was leaving the UK to take up employment overseas, I requested a contract from my prospective employers. Their definition of the word 'contract' meant short-term employment – hence their perplexity when they were offering me permanent and pensionable employment. I was only trying to get an understanding of the terms of our agreement which is another valid definition of the word.

In other situations, employees may be offered temporary contracts while going through a probationary period. This provides a get-out clause for both parties because, once a permanent contract is signed, it becomes difficult to dismiss an unsatisfactory worker.

Interestingly, God's contract in today's text leaves no room for misinterpretation. He set up an arrangement and He did not include a get-out clause for Himself. He promised to be a God to us and the generations following, and He will deliver on His word. He is truth and His word can be trusted. In Him, there is no doubt or shadow of turning. His plan will not change.

I hope you prove Him within your lifetime.

UNFINISHED BUSINESS

I recently had to go into hospital for a booked procedure. Like any person who is preparing to be knocked out, there is always the fear of the unknown. In my case, being a nurse, I know the major complications that can occur even from minor procedures – which can change your future.

Then I got to thinking. My thoughts formed a veritable smorgasbord. Questions flooded my mind faster than I could write them down. What if there are complications? How soon will I be fit for work? How long will I be dependent on my friends and relatives? Then I thought about death, which is the ultimate complication. At least I would not be around to argue with the doctors to see if they made a mistake. The thoughts progressed to my not having enough money to give my family what I would really like to give them. I am not sure if they would really appreciate my taste in books and music. But more importantly, I thought what would be my last words to each of them. I know that they were praying for me and would know that I appreciated their support.

In all this preparation, I was told not to eat anything after midnight. I went around the house, feeling like a convict on death row, wondering what I could treat myself to – my frenzied mind envisaged all my favourite foods. I was now on a roll and this song came to mind:

Verse
Why worry about tomorrow;
Why worry if your steps are getting slow?
If your life is spent lived for Jesus
Then you don't have much farther to go.

Chorus

The next hand you shake could be the hand of the Saviour
The next step you take could be on streets of purest gold.
And your next meal could be the marriage supper
And the next touch you feel – He could be blessing your soul.

My thoughts went to what it would be like to meet Jesus. His would be the next face I see (if I made things right with Him). That is when I asked Him for more of His grace, mercy and time so that I could straighten myself out and have no unfinished business when I meet Him face to face.

INSTRUCTION

"All Scripture is God-breathed and is useful for teaching, rebuking, correcting and training in righteousness ... "
(2 Timothy 3:16, NIV)

Have you ever heard any of the following?

Parent: What's the matter with you? You should know better than that. Don't you know that this thing is dangerous?

Child: But you never told me.

Or

Parent: Haven't I told you not to .... swear? (The blank word being itself an obscenity)

Child: But it's what I always hear you say.

Observe God's modus operandi. He has issued an instruction manual that covers the human code of conduct.

He is gone on to point out what would happen if we did not follow the instructions.

When the consequences of failing to follow the instructions come upon us, He issues rebuke/reproof and reminds us what is expected – instruction in right doing.

He is making all the moves to keep us on the right track. He is just simply amazing. His name be praised!

BURDENS

"Cast all your anxiety on him because he cares for you."
(1 Peter 5:7, NIV)

Brrr, brrr... Brrr, brrr... Brrr, brrr

Mother: Jane, go and get the phone and if it's that Kathy, tell her I'm not in.

Jane: (looking uncomfortable) Mom, I can't do that.

Mother: Just do as I say.

Jane: Hello! Who is it? (Pause)
Just a minute, she was going out; let me see if she's still here.
(Handing over the phone) Mom, it's her!

Mom: (Under her breath) Alright then, give me the phone.

Jane: Hold on! She's coming!

Mom: Kathy, I've got the Health Visitor here, so I can't talk now. Call me later, OK?

Whether by way of apology or justification for her action, the lady explained that although Kathy was her good friend, she always had some problem to moan about and she was not in the mood for listening to her at the moment, as she had her own problems to worry about.

I could not help wondering how many so–called friends groaned silently when they realised who was calling, although talking to the person pleasantly enough; or how many times those with caller ID let the answering machine cut in – just to avoid a difficult caller. Suppose God was like that?

Are you glad that our Father in Heaven tells of His love in the Book He has written? He tells us that He is never tired, so He does not need to slumber or sleep (Psalm 121). That is why we can call on Him at any time and offload our burdens. Just give it a try.

TEAM MEMBERSHIP

"Therefore He is able to save completely those who come to God through Him, because He always lives to intercede for them." (Hebrews 7:25, NIV)

Most girls can remember being part of a group of friends at school. In that group, there would be one particular girl who influenced or determined who joined the group. Everyone wanted to be her friend and a part of her group.

However, the price of membership was unfailing loyalty. This meant that if she fell out with someone, or disliked them for any reason that took her fancy; her loyal subjects did not dare talk to them either, for fear of being expelled from the group.

Now, just suppose our friend, Jesus, was like that. Imagine how many times He would have fallen out with us. We would have only one chance to mess up – because after that it would be expulsion from His team.

Thankfully, we only need to tell Him we are sorry for doing something wrong and He will intercede with the Father, so that we are reinstated and our record is cleared as if we had never sinned. That is what He lives to do. It is all part of His job description. Remember one of His titles is Repairer of the breach. Therefore, do not be afraid to confess and ask forgiveness to stay on His team (1 John 1:9).

WORSHIP

THE LIGHT

"Thy Word is a lamp unto my feet, and a light unto my path."
(Psalm 119:105)

Ouch! I just stepped on something. It felt like the heel of a shoe that was not where it should be. I was stepping gingerly on that foot when I bumped into something else. It was the bowl with leftovers from my midnight feast of popcorn. You guessed right, I had put it at the side of the bed with the intention of moving it in the morning. But I was heading to the bathroom in the dark. All these bumps and pains would have been avoided – except that I was too sleepy, as well as lazy, to turn on the light. I am sure you have been there.

On reflection, that is how the journey of life seems at times – full of bumps, scrapes, potholes, etc. The traveller in our text is here expressing appreciation for the provision made for this journey. He is not alone, and nothing is left to chance. The imagery provided here, implies travel through a dark place. Yet the traveller is provided with adequate light to ensure that he travels in safety. If he follows the light, there is no chance of stumbling, falling, tripping up, or bumping into objects. This light is bright enough to illuminate the path – not just for the far distance, but for the next footstep (one step at a time).

It would appear as if the traveller has very little to do, except to follow the light. I get the impression that the traveller may not be very familiar with the path or the destination. Each step is a step into the unknown. The landmarks are similar, but different, at each phase of the journey. So, the traveller really has to be willing to be guided by the Light – which is in itself an expression of faith in the Light source. I am reminded of the children of Israel as they journeyed through the wilderness. They did not know where they were going, other than they followed the Light, which was the pillar of cloud by day and the pillar of fire by night. It was only when they came up *to* the Red Sea that they realised where they were. Yet, it was still that Light that led them *through* the Red Sea.

As Christians or followers of Christ, we have made a commitment to follow the path that He has mapped out for us. That means that even though we will not know the way, we would have purposed in our hearts to follow Him anyhow. Therefore, it is not enough to know of the Word, but our obligation is to demonstrate our knowledge, by practicing what we know. In practical terms, this means plugging in and switching on.

So while we do not require the human trappings of a map or compass for this journey, each one of us can successfully complete it because the Lord, our Guide, has not only walked the road already, but He is willing to walk it with us and be the Light to prevent us from falling (into sin, that is). As this is a personal encounter, each traveller has an opportunity to seek the help of the Guide who is ever present, ever able and ever willing to deliver us from all evil.

Interestingly, although this is an individual reflection, it is important that I acknowledge other travellers along the journey to the Kingdom – especially as we enter at different stages and proceed at different paces. I must appreciate that my progress may serve as a witness to other travellers – especially when I encounter what would appear to be obstacles, setbacks, diversions or difficulties. My life can either be an example or stumbling block.

Great things happen when we pray and study God's Word – we are plugged into the greatest Light source possible, and our lights shine brighter than we could have dreamed possible. After the dark, unconscious hours of sleep, we need to connect to our Light Source for guidance through the uncharted hours of each new day by taking a daily dose from His Word.

Try it and you will see!

POWERFUL WORDS

"Through faith we understand that the worlds were framed by the Word of God, so that things which are seen were not made of things which do appear." (Hebrews 11:3)

I remember when we did Cookery at school. It was called Home Economics then. I now understand why. At some point in the term, we each had to prepare a menu, go shopping with a limited budget and prepare the meal within a 3-hour morning session.

For some, their money finished and certain essential ingredients were forgotten, or they did not buy enough of a certain item that was common to several dishes. Others, with less time management skills, still had things to do when the time was up and, in between times, each of us had an accident of some sort. One dropped an egg, one almost caused an explosion by turning the the heat too high under a pan of oil, and another broke the Pyrex dish borrowed from her mother.

Teachers were invited to sample and judge our creations. Invariably, something either had too much or too little salt, or a cake had fallen in. Afterwards, we were allowed to tuck in. We definitely left full – too full to concentrate for a double period of Math in the afternoon.

Now, I am reminded of Creation. Can you imagine God with several mounds of soil and different bales of grass? Suppose He forgot the colouring for the flowers or turned the heat too high for the sunshine. Thankfully, we do not have to imagine anything. He only had to say the word and all that we now enjoy came forth – fully and correctly formed. What we can not imagine is the state of perfection that existed back then, because things have since been tainted – although there is a lot of beauty still around. He did not have any accidents or have to throw out one mixture to start again. No wonder after each creation day God looked at His work and said it was very good.

Since He holds all the wealth of the world in His hands and all He did was talk the world into existence, then I only need to make a request and He will commission an angel to deliver what I need – once it is His will to let me have it. Could it be that I do not have more because I have not been asking?

As we were not around to appreciate the original beauty of creation, He has promised us a new home in a restored version of Eden. He is preparing it even now, and when He is finished, He will say the word for Jesus to come and get us. The God we serve is powerful and His words bear evidence to this. So be ready for Him to perform his transformation in your life and prepare for His eternal company. You only need to submit and His power will do the rest.

WIND

"The wind blows wherever it pleases. You hear its sound, but you cannot tell where it comes from or where it is going. So it is with everyone born of the Spirit."
(John 3:8, NIV)

No one has ever seen the wind, but you can tell its direction and its effect. You only know that it is there. Have you ever known it not to be there?

I once heard a friend say that they were stuck in a sailboat between two islands because the sea was becalmed. That means the wind, upon which the sails were dependent, was not blowing and so the boat sat there in the middle of the sea – incapable of movement.

The passengers and crew must have been frustrated – the passengers because they wanted to reach their destination; the crew because, with increasing emphasis on quality and penalty clauses written in small print, their company may have been liable to pay compensation for late arrival – all due to circumstances beyond their control.

In contrast, the wind can be powerful and this reminds me of the effects of the Holy Spirit.

God the Holy Spirit is ever present – never absent or taking a rest. Even when He seems calm, He is speaking to us. He advises us to be still and know God, our Father (Psalm 46:10). He says that we must just wait and see what He can do for us (Exodus 14:13). What is more, you will never be the same when He has finished with you. Remember when the Holy Spirit appeared through the sound of a mighty rushing wind – how the unlearned disciples were rendered eloquent and fluent in foreign languages on the day of Pentecost – so much so that the religious leaders marvelled and asked, "Aren't those the Galileans?" (Acts 2:1-7).

In the quiet times of our lives, when alone with our thoughts and memories – whether they are peaceful or stormy – we can be assured that God is very present in the form of the Holy Spirit, inviting us to take His hand and receive strength.

I am reminded that God the Holy Spirit communicates with us in various ways (1 Kings 19:11,12). Please tune in so that you can hear His voice and feel His impact on your life!

JOY

"I rejoiced with those who said to me, 'Let us go to the house of the Lord.'" (Psalm 122:1, NIV)

I can distinctly recall the pleasure on my colleague's face when she revealed that she was going to the Robbie Williams concert. Then her expression became incredulous when I said that I was not going. She said, 'I can't believe you live so close and aren't going!' That is because I lived within walking distance from the venue. She went on to declare that there was no way she was going to miss this chance of a lifetime.

People came from all over the country. Some arrived from midday the previous day. On the day, the volume of vehicles and pedestrians made it very difficult for people going elsewhere to get through, as the main roads were jammed. And, of course, it ended very late at night, as it was the subject of every conversation at work the following day.

Contrast this to the attendance at church. Very rarely is there a traffic jam en-route to the car park and less frequently is there standing room only. Even more rarely do we leave with a glow on our faces as if we met someone special.

The psalmist, David, said he was glad when they (possibly his parents) said to him, "Let us go into the house of the Lord!" (Psalm 122:1). I hope that we realise that God's presence is in His house and the time we spend with Him is special.

God invites you to a concert – entry is free; the tickets are already paid for. Everyone is welcome and all can contribute because everyone can testify of His goodness to them – whether by psalms, hymns or spiritual songs.

You will certainly leave with a glow in your heart and on your face. Remember how Moses' face shone when He came from receiving the Commandments on Mount Sinai (Exodus 33:18 – 34:30). And he had only seen God's back. Your invitation is ready.

Robbie Williams' fans can sing along with him because they know his songs; they have bought his CDs; they listened to him on the radio. You and I can sing of Jesus' love because we are in tune with Him – in our morning and evening worship and throughout the day. We do not have to go anywhere because wherever we lift up our hearts to Him becomes a place of worship.

WOW!

Wow! Can you believe it?

Believe what?

I passed my exams! I still can't believe it!

I guess you have had similar experiences where something has happened that you find hard to believe. I wonder why there was this incredulous response when we prayed about the matter. Was it that we did not really believe God would come through or that we expected him to do less? Was our response a reflection of the extent of our faith?

Faith is exercised or demonstrated when we continue to believe even when there is nothing to base that belief upon. It is letting go and letting God show us how well He operates in extreme circumstances.

Letting go of what though? It seems as if we hold on to doubts, or limit God by our experiences. It is hard to completely believe when we have that niggling feeling at the back of our minds that things may not work out, especially knowing some unfortunate outcomes on things previous.

I have learned to say, Thanks in advance to God – in anticipation of a blessing. For example, I go to the City Centre, the parking lot looks full and I do not have enough change for the Pay and Display meter. I consciously whisper a prayer asking for a space and when I have almost circled the entire parking lot – mentally resigning myself to having to go elsewhere, I see someone opening his or her car door, or just pulling out. What can I say, but "Wow!"

There are other times when I consciously say to the Lord that I will still love Him even if there is no space, because my love for Him is not dependent on something as small as a parking space. He does not have to prove Himself to me. I only have to accept that it was best for me not to park there at that time. Remember, His ways are not our ways and His thoughts are not our thoughts. So be prepared to say "Wow!" the next time you ask God for a favour.

MYSTERY

"O the depth of the riches both of the wisdom and knowledge of God! How unsearchable are His judgments, and His ways past finding out!" (Romans 11:33)

"Can't you wait?"

"No!"

"Strange?"

"Nah..."

I am talking about my habit of reading the end of a story before the beginning. Whether detective, court scene, mystery or romance, I am a believer in happy endings, and I want the bad guys to get their just deserts. So, when the suspense gets too much, I just tell myself that they do not know what is coming.

On reflection, that is the way the story of our lives unfolds. God, as the author – knowing the end from the beginning – says, 'Wait and see!' Despite your difficulties at the moment, there is a good outcome awaiting you. Unlike storytelling, however, it is not possible to jump ahead in time to see how the plot ends. It will remain a mystery that only God can fathom.

Our only comfort is to hold God's hand as He leads us through the various scenes of our lives. He assures us that His thoughts for us are of peace, not of evil and to give us an expected end (Jeremiah 29:11); and He who began a good work in you will complete it until the day of Jesus Christ (Philippians 1:6). You see, we have until Jesus comes to have our puzzles solved. Yes, they will be solved, because He who promised is faithful (Hebrews 10:23). So, hold on!